# The Clash.
# Photographs by Bob Gruen.

**Edited by Chris Salewicz.**
**Design by Form.**

CW01021970

# Introduction

The Clash were a very visual group in the sense that they were aware of the whole look - the show, the clothes, the act. Everything about the group looked like art - their backdrops were always very important - the stage had to be saying something… so you'd get, for example, a squadron of bombers looking as though they were about to fly out over the group onstage.

Joe Strummer is a very animated performer, dropping to his knees or gripping his hand against his forehead - very dramatic. Paul Simonon is the best-looking guy ever in rock'n' roll and Mick Jones is also a very spectacular performer. When he and Paul would run across the stage in opposite directions jumping in the air, it looked absolutely amazing. When you were taking pictures of them, it was hard to anticipate what they were going to do next.

I had fantastic access to the group. I managed to become just a natural part of the situation: I'd turn up with my cameras and say, 'Can I get a few shots?' And I could get it all in ten minutes.

I came to London in October 1976. Vivienne Westwood and Caroline Coon took me to see The Clash; it was their second show at the ICA and I got a couple of pictures. I thought they were very powerful and exciting. I didn't come back to London until about twelve months later. I called up CBS, their record company, to find out what they were doing. CBS wasn't interested: 'The Clash are out of control - we can't work with them.' But they told me the

group were playing in Glasgow that night. So I flew up there. As I walked into the hotel, Mick and Paul were standing at the desk. Mick said, 'You're that guy from New York.' And Paul added, 'Look out for us, because we're cunts.' 'You look it,' I said. And we became friends from then on.

Their music wasn't just about being angry, but on a higher level than that, really examining things and suggesting solutions. In the midst of a rocking set, you would suddenly get a lengthy stretch of dub which would provide time for emotional introspection on the subject matter.

The Clash seemed far more serious than any other groups I'd encountered - it was as though they were genuinely trying to figure out what was going on and what to do about it. I was immediately impressed with how open they were to meeting their fans - they'd give their maximum attention to any yobbo, and if he still had more to say, he'd be very welcome to come back to the hotel to continue the debate. They reached out to the fans to do the things that they wished bands had done for them. That's why they always talked to the fans after the show and went out of their way to know them and be available to them.

Other bands would hire bodyguards to keep the fans away, yet The Clash would hire people to get the fans in and often argue with the security of the venue who had been employed to prevent people sneaking in. The Clash would say,

'They're not sneaking in - we're bringing them in. Yes: all fifty of these people are coming into our dressing-room.' At Shea Stadium they had this line of about 150 people, and Kosmo Vinyl was saying, 'Yes, they're coming back to the dressing room!' And the security guards had been hired specifically to see that would never happen. They always made it happen - they never forgot what it was like to be a fan. As commercial as The Clash got it never really seemed to be about the money. That's why for their opening acts they brought people like Bo Diddley and Lee Dorsey along. They were fans of these people.

The Clash were the real thing, the only band that mattered; they were the best one, a band who never forgot their roots. They cared about their audience and tried to give them a good show with a moral conscience and a lot of fun. For me they were fantastic to work with.

Bob Gruen
New York 2001

# Thank you

I very much appreciate the support of all the people who helped put this book together. First, of course, The Clash themselves: Joe Strummer, Mick Jones, Paul Simonon, Topper Headon.

There was always a large cast of characters around The Clash, all of whom were equally important. Many of them have provided vital information for this book.

Specifically, I should like to thank: writer extraordinaire Chris Salewicz, who gathered and edited the text for this book;  Malcolm McLaren and Vivienne Westwood, who took me to Club Louise and introduced me to English punks; painter and sometime Clash manager Caroline Coon, who first took me to see The Clash; punk inspiration and Clash manager Bernard Rhodes; Clash mouthpiece Kosmo Vinyl; tour manager Johnny Green; band protector Raymond Jordan; band assistant Baker; photographer Sheila Rock, who gave me a place to stay in England; powerhouse publicist Susan Blond, who made it possible for me to travel with the band; rock writer Lisa Robinson, who as editor of Rock Scene magazine gave me a reason to shoot so many of my photos; punk poet and writer Richard Hell; filmmaker Don Letts; rockin' disc jockey Barry 'Scratchy' Myers; the inimatable Patti Paladin; photographer Kate Simon and singer David Johansen; Mandi Newall, who helps me collect my thoughts; my photo-agent Virginia Lohle of Star File Photo; my assistant Karla Merrifield, who kept me organised through the Seventies and Eighties; my studio manager

Linda Rowe, who printed the photos in this book; my family and my mother who taught me photography; and especially my fabulous wife Elizabeth who keeps me together.

Philip Salon and Malcolm McLaren outside
Club Louise in Soho's Poland Street (formerly
Chagaramas, a leading soul club), October 1976.

Top, Joe, Soo Catwoman, Mick and Marco Peroni.
Bottom, Paul Cook, Paul Simonon and friends.

**Soo Catwoman:** I didn't know I was part of a revolution - I was just doing what I felt.

**Caroline Coon:** I'm working, doing one of those journalist-all-through-the-night writing stints. And the doorbell goes at midnight, and I get off the typewriter, and there's this gang. I don't want to let them in - I'm working, I have copy to deliver. The woman whose flat I was staying in was away. So I thought I'd take them into her room. Then I made a cup of tea for them, but I didn't want them there. I'm trying to get rid of them.

Top, Soo Catwoman and Joe.
Bottom, Caroline Coon, Johnny Rotten, Soo,
Debbie and Joe.

On Saturday, 23 October 1976, The Clash headlined a show at London's ICA, the Institute for Contemporary Arts. Also on the bill were Subway Sect and Snatch, featuring Judy Nylon and Patti Paladin.

Shane MacGowan, a noted punk 'face', was entwined with "Mad" Jane, later of The Modettes; only when blood began to stream down his face and neck did he realise that in her passion she had bitten off most of an earlobe. (Within the culture of punk, this was held to be a rather impressive statement of primal art). The incident gave The Clash their first significant music press coverage. "Without Mad Jane's teeth and Shane's earlobe, we wouldn't have got in the papers that week," said Strummer.

**Mick:** That was the night of Shane McGowan's earlobe, wasn't it? He didn't really have it bitten off, you know. Isn't that the same show where Patti Smith got up on stage during our set?

**Paul:** That was the ICA - it was called A Night of Pure Energy. My haircut's gone very mod; it had flopped down from all the jumping around onstage. In the beginning all that jumping about was a way of dodging gob and missiles generally. There's Joe with his sharks' teeth - when I first met him they looked just like real sharks' teeth.

Joe: You should put in as many as you can where people are smiling. Because when you do a photo-shoot you tend to stand around looking pissed off.

Mick: That's the Glasgow Apollo. It was such a big drop from the stage, wasn't it? Really high.

Paul: I remember early on we had a backdrop of an old lady sitting in an armchair, and the other one was a Messerschmidt. I remember Mick being a bit perturbed because we always used to refer to the old lady as Mick's Nan, with whom he used to live at first. For the backdrops we used to go through reggae albums and get the images reduced to black and white and have them blown up. At first we experimented with film projectors, but there was so much going on already onstage that we found a still image was much more powerful than a moving one: for a group that doesn't move maybe moving images are quite handy. Much later we also tried banks of TV screens, but that had the same problem.

**Paul:** It was quite frightening looking down at the Apollo, because it was quite a drop. So you had to be quite careful. Unfortunately gob did still land on the stage, even at that distance. It did make the stage rather slippery - it was like an ice-rink.

After that show I was done by the police for 'attempting to rescue a prisoner', which was an unusual thing to be done for. That and drunk and disorderly - but I wasn't drunk, not at all, because we'd just done a show.

I pretty much just ran over and threw myself on top of Joe - they were laying him down with a truncheon. That was just a nightmare, that gig. What we didn't know was that there was an ongoing war between the bouncers and the people who go to the concerts - a running battle. Because of all the friction in the Apollo, we'd verbally had a go at the bouncers, and then it turned out that the bouncers were after us. So we had to get out of the venue fast. As soon as we were outside one of the fans had a real go at Joe about the bouncers, violence. And out of complete frustration he threw a lemonade bottle on the ground. And that was that: the police came from nowhere and started hitting him. That's why I went over to dive on top of him.

Then when I was being dragged into the police car one of them went, 'Where you from?' 'London.' B-I-F-F: straight in my face. 'Well, this is Glasgow.' I suppose that's what you'd call a Glasgow kiss.

We got herded into the main area in the station, and all our audience were in there as well. Fortunately, me and Joe got put in the same cell. Throughout the night the fans were singing Clash songs like 'The Prisoner'. Because we had these trousers that had millions of pockets, the police got fed up going through them. Joe actually had some speed in one of them, so we did it and were up all night with these fans singing.

The next morning we were taken into the holding-room at the court with all the other prisoners, and the guard was saying, 'What's up with you lot? You must have gone soft.' Because they hadn't beaten us up because we were English. But everyone was really nice to us: they gave us cigarettes - and these weren't our fans, just drunks from the night before. I remember Joe being told off for saying 'your honour' to the magistrate - you had to say 'sir'. We were fined about £30 each, and then it was on to Aberdeen.

**Mick:** Corky (Dave Cork, top left, between Joe and Paul) was one of the promoters. He was the one who was always last on the coach - 'Come on, let's go quickly!' - just as the hotel manager is coming out of the hotel saying: 'Here, what about this?'

**Paul:** Corky had to deal with Bernie all the time, which probably drained the life force out of his body. Look, there's Corky practising, looking like a member of an American group in the mid-70s.

**Bob:** We were staying at this nice, quaint English countryside hotel, instead of a brick motel. It has formal gardens. But they didn't like the look of us when we arrived. 'What? The Clash? A group? No way!' And so Corky spent half an hour persuading them to let the band stay, promising there would be no problems with the fans. And so the whole band was trying to behave like good schoolboys. Everybody was pretty tired and went to sleep quickly. Except for Corky who was so stressed, he flipped out and went down and wrecked the whole lobby, throwing couches and tables. Raymond, who worked with the group, came and got me because I'd been travelling with Corky in the car. I had to talk to him, but I didn't even know the guy. I'm sitting there and Corky is crying like a baby. He has his head in my lap and I'm trying to console him: 'There, there: it'll be all right.' He's going: 'Everybody wants me to take care of everything.'

**Mick (laughs):** But that was his job! Sorry.

**Paul:** One thing that amazed Kosmo Vinyl later on was how I used to drink those large cartons of milk in America. I used to drink about a quarter of the milk and pour cognac and Kahlua in and then shake it up. Kosmo for ages thought I was drinking just milk, until he tried it, which gave him a real shock.

**How long did you wear those tops?**

**Paul:** Not long, just one tour really. It was so hot onstage because of the lights that it seemed a suitable thing to wear. When you used to play places like Liverpool Eric's the ceiling would rain because of the condensation. I just fixed it together: it was made from military netting that you'd get from Lawrence Corner in London. I stitched it together.

**Richard Hell:** This is a good example of how pictures lie, because I think it looks fascinating and even glamorous, when in fact it depicts something horrible and dull. I'm kind of kidding (it actually looks horrible and dull - no, I didn't mean that... uh... or horrible and dull is fascinating... where am I...) No, but that's really my reaction: Wow, we look so cute, who'd ever guess how miserable it really was. I mean Mick was fine I'm sure, but Bob Quine was resenting me and hating the moronic English 'Punk' scene, and I was exhausted and sick from discovering what it means to have a heroin habit while also frustrated at the drag of having to play for British Clash fans every night. I had mixed feelings about the English punk scene. It was kind of humiliating to be in a position of playing for an audience that was there to cheer for a band that was basically built out of what we'd created (we being the Ramones and me and the Dolls, and the New York scene around 1974 to '76), but at the same time I could see what got people in England excited. What the hell else did they have to be excited about?

**Mick:** The guy in the blue shirt (top left) is Lester Bangs. He was on holiday with us for a bit: he wrote this enormous article in the NME. He was one of the featured characters in the film Almost Famous: he was the voice of reason.

**Paul:** Lester was good fun, a nice character.

**Bob:** One thing for me was that this was where The Who's Live at Leeds was recorded, and I thought, 'At last: here I am!' But the venue was so corny-looking - it looked like a lunch-room, which in fact it was. There were funny lights and linoleum on the floor. But at one point I remember Joe going, 'No more Queen Elizabeth!' And they all cheered. And 'No more Rolling Stones or Beatles!' And they all cheered. And then he said, 'But John Lennon rules, OK?' And they cheered. And I thought, 'How does John manage to escape?'

**Bob:** To me it was important to show how much the band were in touch with their fans and how people dressed like them. And how they would have as many fans come backstage as they wanted to.

**Paul:** The weird thing is that I remember at the ICA, me and Joe were trying to work out how everyone spoke to Mick and not to us, and we thought there must be something wrong with us. So one day we went over to Mick and he said, 'Oh, it's because they're scared of you.' In some ways I then took that on board and I just used to generally scowl a lot. 'Cos I remember Joe being surrounded by people who wanted to talk politics, and Joe had just come offstage. And I looked around at Joe and saw him drowning in political rhetoric. And I was quite pleased I got out of that.

**Bob:** I remember how even at Shea Stadium there was always a crowd around after the show. Kosmo would line them up, and then they'd come in. I never saw any other band do that. Kosmo would deal with security and insist, 'These kids are coming in the dressing-room.' Everyone else hires people to keep them out.

**Paul:** At times we'd have a lot of conflict with the venue owners: they weren't used to this novel approach.

July 1978

Joe: I like to make instant decisions and go the whole hog with them. Because when I was young I remember reading about the Cherokees. I read some book about Indians, and one sentence was that when a Cherokee is faced with a decision, he always takes the more reckless alternative. And I always thought, 'Go for it: what's life for but to make reckless decisions.'

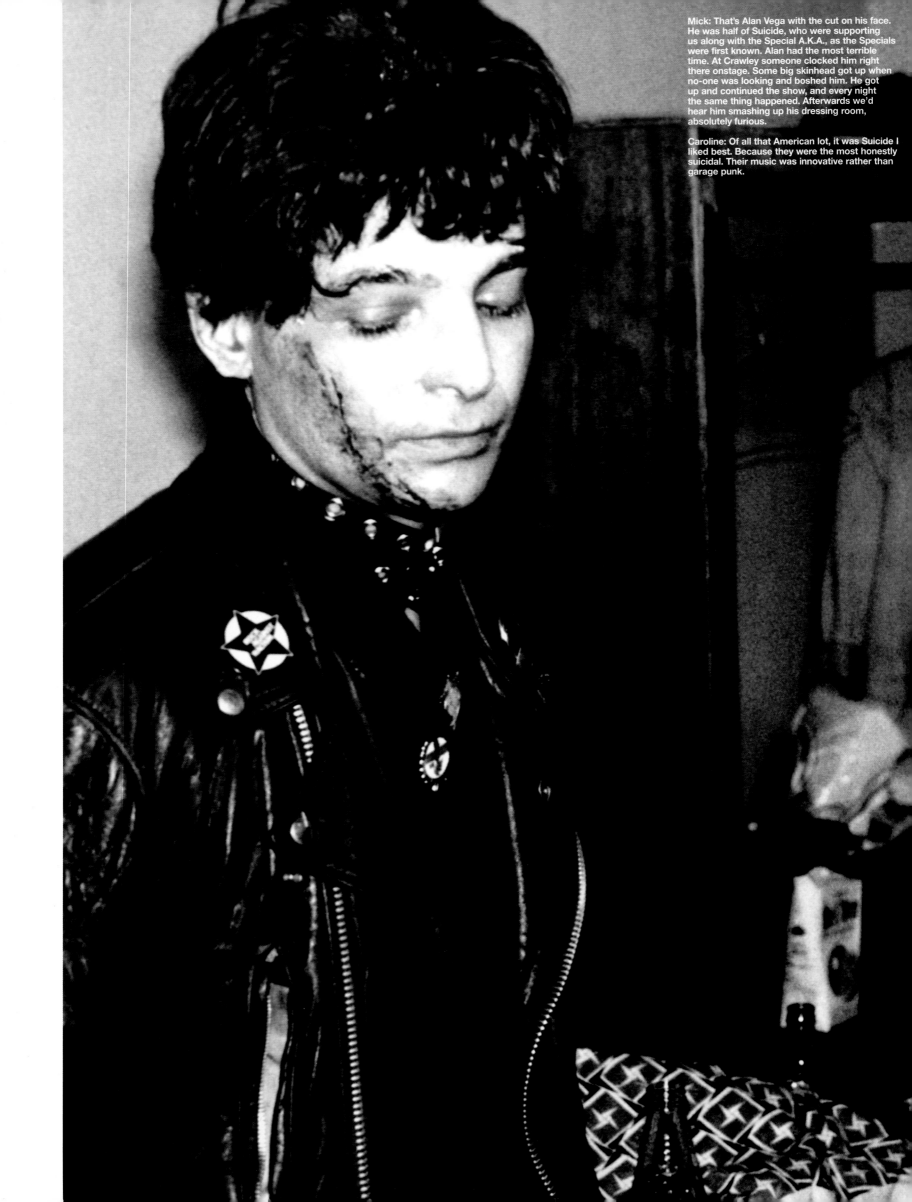

Mick: That's Alan Vega with the cut on his face. He was half of Suicide, who were supporting us along with the Special A.K.A., as the Specials were first known. Alan had the most terrible time. At Crawley someone clocked him right there onstage. Some big skinhead got up when no-one was looking and boshed him. He got up and continued the show, and every night the same thing happened. Afterwards we'd hear him smashing up his dressing room, absolutely furious.

Caroline: Of all that American lot, it was Suicide I liked best. Because they were the most honestly suicidal. Their music was innovative rather than garage punk.

In September 1978, The Clash came to
New York to mix their second album at
the Record Plant.

Mick, Joe and Sandy Pearlman, producer of
Give 'em Enough Rope.

**Mick:** Joe and I were in San Francisco, working on the second album. It was the first time we'd been to America, before we came to tour. Sandy Pearlman took us to his favourite studio in San Francisco and we worked there for three weeks, just Joe and me. We were asking if Paul and Topper could come over, and they're saying, 'Oh, I don't know.' It was when things were up in the air - when Bernie had just gone for the first time.

We had a week off after we'd finished our recording - we were going to mix it at the Record Plant in New York, at 44th and 8th. We said, 'We've got to have the other two over here, they've got to come.' We said, 'We'll meet them in New York.' Joe drove across country in a flatbed truck and I went to LA for a week. My first time in LA: I went with Sandy, because Blue Oyster Cult, who he managed and produced, were playing there.

But when Sandy and I arrived in LA, I found we were staying at one of those airport hotels. And Sandy goes, 'Right, I'm going to the gig, I'll see you later.' And I'm, 'Hang on a minute: fuck this - I'm off.' And I got a cab and checked in at the Tropicana on Santa Monica and La Cienega in West Hollywood. Then I went to the gig - it must have been at the Coliseum because everyone working there was all dressed as Romans - I was amazed. So this is the group with Sandy and engineer 'Corky' Stasiak at the Record Plant.

**Paul:** Cor, that album was a bloody nightmare to make. Sandy Pearlman was so particular that each track had to be done a million times each. It was really draining. It sounds laboured. The first album was done in a couple of weekends. So it was like going from one extreme to the other. Of course, after this we did London Calling with Guy Stevens, which was completely emotionally charged.

**Mick and Paul discuss Bob's suntan.**

**Bob:** I liked to look healthy at that time. I'd stay up all night, run around town working all day, but in the morning I would lay on the dock to get some sun and cure the hangover.

John Lennon had made this guitar for an avant-garde festival a couple of years earlier and had stored it at the Record Plant.

**Paul:** It reminds me of those Mexican basses, the acoustic mariachi ones.

VALUE SMALL PRIZES FOR LARGER PRIZE

Joe rests between tracks on the couch at the Record Plant. Bob had previously taken a picture of John Lennon in exactly the same position.

Bob. We went down to Little Italy to try to get
something to eat, but everywhere was closed.
So we went to the deli and bought spaghetti and
sauce and went back to my apartment and ate
it and watched New York Dolls videos I'd made.
You can see the packet of spaghetti on top of my
car, a '54 Buick.

**November 1978.**

**Bob:** This was back in England.

**Paul:** I used to get these pieces of felt and match them up to colours. The idea behind a lot of the Clash stage stuff was just to be practical. The Pistols had the straps between the legs of their bondage trousers, which we thought was potentially a liability if you're trying to run away from somebody. So having all the zips and pockets simply made it more practical. I spent a lot of time with Alex Michon who was the girl

who used to make them up. I suppose I had more of a hand in that department, because of my art school background, especially with the earlier painted stuff - the drip Jackson Pollock, Rauschenberg business.

We'd do stuff like put the shirt pockets on the wrong side. It was based on all the Lawrence Corner stuff, because that's where I used to do my shopping. We didn't have a shop like the Pistols had. So necessity became the mother of invention, as they say. The bright colours thing was like the name 'Clash' - a clash of colours.

**Joe:** That scene in Spinal Tap, my favourite film, where he's complaining about the sandwiches, is serious too. I don't think we did anything as stupid as that, but it's in the ballpark. Somehow you become so stressed out. This is why I think rock singers or opera singers have tantrums: so many things are demanded of you that you've got nothing left to give. But there's no stopping the demanding, and you overboil. Some circuit fuses, and you start complaining that the smoked salmon doesn't fit the bread, and throwing a fit about nothing.

**Joe:** Mick, how do I get F sharp?

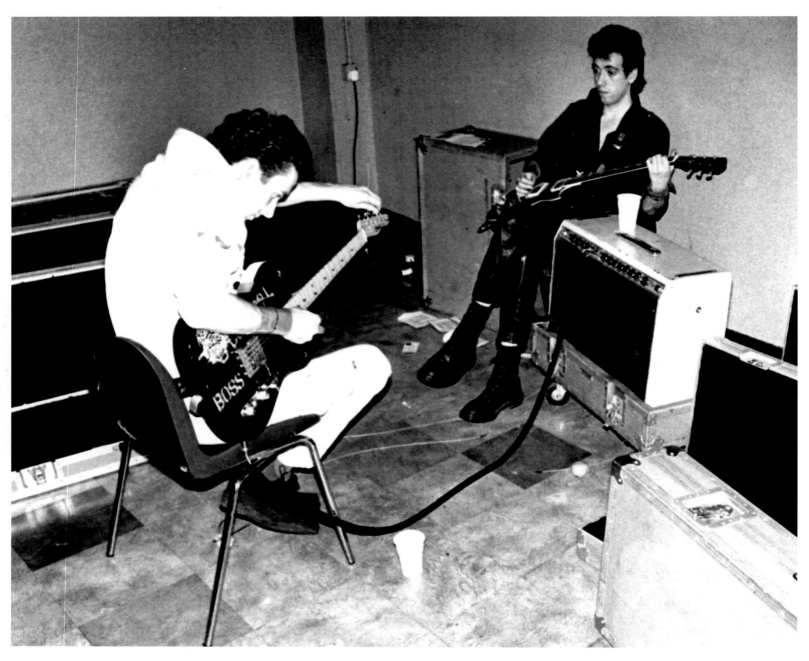

Paul: That's Caroline and a bottle of Simonon Comfort, as Strummer used to call Southern Comfort. Delicious, that drink.

In Feburary 1979 The Clash set off on their first American tour.

Caroline: Part of the punk ethic was to refuse to be in any way gracious to anyone from the record company who came backstage. My charm helped a bit, especially when we ran out of money halfway through the tour, and I had to go on my knees to the record company and ask for more cash to finish the tour. But they did it because The Clash were playing fantastic gigs that were absolute sell-outs.

You have to understand that The Clash never ever did a gig that wasn't rampacked. From the first gig they ever did in London. Because of the build-up, with everyone knowing there was something happening. Unlike the Pistols who for the first few gigs were building the punk audience. By the time The Clash came along there was already quite a big scene, so they never ever had to do a gig where they had to win over the audience. The audience was so ready and up for it. I don't think there's been any band in the history of rock'n'roll that has had that experience. Even the Beatles, the Rolling Stones had to build an audience. But the audience was there for The Clash, ready for it.

Bob: The Clash liked America in general. Coming from England, the whole country seems like Disneyland. That's what America does well: we are big and bright and candy-coloured and pink and yellow and "red, white and blue". You come to America and it's fast food and fast girls and fast cars and big, wide-open streets. In America anyone says anything to anybody - pretty loudly. The band really liked that swaggering American attitude and the big cars.

**Mick:** That's the border at Vancouver, hence the checked lumberjack shirt.

**Paul:** Everyone had emptied their pockets of millions of knives etc. that they thought were not allowable. It looks like we're hanging out with two Western locals, but that's Johnny Green, our tour manager, on the right, and Baker, one of our longstanding roadies, on the left.

**Bob:** I flew up to Vancouver. They had already been there rehearsing for a couple of days. The first show of the tour was in Vancouver. I remember everyone being really nervous about whether they would be searched at the border: 'Would the band be harassed?' They all psyched up for it. Then no-one even looked at them at immigration.

**Caroline:** We're bombing through the southern States late at night. I used to sit up front with the driver during these long all-night drives, checking he wasn't falling asleep. Suddenly there's the sound of a police siren. So the driver pulls over and the cop says, 'You're speeding: all out!'

But the driver is an experienced rock'n'roll driver. He gets out of the cab and says, 'I would sure like to empty everybody out, but I've got Dolly Parton in the back.' So the cop says, 'Oh, sorry, sir, for stopping you: drive on.' Respect to the queen of the South, Dolly Parton.

On the bus the film that they are showing, which we see time and time again, is the first Star Wars movie. This bus actually had been Dolly Parton's bus, so we had good movies, but the one they always went back to was Star Wars.

**Paul:** That was our first experience of tour buses. It was OK - this particular bus was quite nice, because Bo Diddley used to sit up all night and put his guitar in the bunk instead. Which was unusual.

**Joe:** I like this because it shows what the bedding was like. You think, 'Well, if I was on that bus it looks pretty comfy.' And you can see the set-up. Also, that guy there is Ace Penna, the tour manager, and he worked hard. We drove him to the end of his tether.

Joe: On the road you get so used to sudden things happening and nothing fazes you. And I realised that if a bomb went off and three people dived through the window, my reaction would be zero. I might swivel my head slowly. That's what you realise when you're on the road, and not to worry about it. If a stage collapses and a lighting rig falls on it, then I realise I might not be able to do the gig. You don't jump at the first thing. You keep your energy for what it's for.

**Paul:** Essential Clash luggage - guitar and giant cassette machine.

**Bob:** People don't understand how the rest of life in a group isn't all the fun of being onstage. You see a group performing, and a bunch of girls wanting to talk to them, and you think, 'This is the life!' But the lonely days and nights when you don't get a chance to have a bite to eat and there are a lot of people who you don't know wanting to know you - well, it's just not like being comfortable and hanging with your friends.

**Bob:** They'd all been in New York and really liked it and now they were getting the whole American experience. It was a bit subdued at first, because they came over the border and there was this excitement about being in America. But it was a long ride: driving from Vancouver to San Francisco was two days. We stopped overnight in Seattle. Topper wanted to go see Bruce Lee's grave, his big karate/kung fu pilgrimage. I remember the very first morning in America we got our wake-up calls and the news that Sid Vicious was dead. Sid was kind of a sweet kid. Things were quiet and subdued for the rest of the ride down to San Francisco.

**Joe:** This is Frisco, right? That wild show we did for that new youth movement… a charity show for this youth organisation. It was kind of like a squatters' beatnik neighbourhood scenario, this.

**Bob:** In San Francisco the group played a benefit gig for the homeless. There was a lot of trouble with Bill Graham over that - Graham was promoting the official San Francisco concert, but they had this alternative gig going on as well. It's interesting that the first show The Clash played in the USA was a benefit.

**Caroline:** Part of the policy in every town to which we went - and to persuade the record company of this was a nightmare - was to play a benefit gig for whichever youth group in the town needed a benefit, and then do the commercial gig. We tried to do it as often as possible, and get the local bands to play as well.

**Mick:** We played a benefit at the Temple, next door to Jim Jones's temple - the guy who went out to take Kool Aid with his followers in Guyana. There was lots of trouble with that, because Bill Graham didn't want us to do it. It was great that night.

When we first went to San Francisco, Joe and I, we went to that place where we played the benefit, and it was like the last vestiges of a real hippie night: with a little imagination you could see what it must have been like.

There was an American hippie group called Stoneground who came over to England and played at the Roundhouse where I used to go every Sunday to an event called Implosion. I used to look forward to it all week when I was at school. I used to go there and idiot-dance, in the days before I'd worked out what I really liked. And if you look at the back of Stoneground's album there's a picture of them onstage at the Roundhouse. And there's me at the front, doing an idiot-dance. I've got really long hair.

I also had a colour photo of me in the first fifteen rows of the Stones free concert in Hyde Park in 1969 - it had taken me all day to get up to the front.

Did it seem different playing in the States
from the UK?

Paul: Yeah. For a start there was no gobbing.
That was a big plus, because clothes tended
to last longer. I suppose people were trying
to figure out what the whole thing was about
from what they'd read in the press about punk
groups in London.

Joe: Me, Lemmy, Rod Stewart, we're in another medium, where the singing is rough, and there's nothing wrong with rough singing. People must like it: it must have a message of soul in it. Who can say what singing is? People understand that you're out there, and you're going to come back with some strange murmuring or whimpering from where you've been in your thoughts.

That's what singing is. You're relating some emotional experiences you had... that you shouldn't have had if you wanted to retain your sanity. With singing you don't have to think about it.

What was it about The Clash that created that positive energy that swirled around them like an aura?

Bob: The level of intelligence is very high, and the jokes and the comments weren't just stupid and silly and they weren't just looking for girls. They wanted a good time, but they seemed to have a social conscience and an awareness. They were very aware of what was going on, but also having fun.

They weren't apathetic - they were concerned, but not pedantic about it. The level with The Clash was high - the jokes were higher; they would relate to several levels of things. It wasn't just let's-get-drunk-and-fuck, like most bands. Each one of them was spot-on and intelligent and aware. Their eyes were open and they saw what was going on and then they'd make a joke of it.

How did people respond to them at first in America? Did they get it?

Bob: Oh yeah. They hadn't seen them, but people had heard the record by then. There was a vibe going about them. I think all of the shows were sold out.

The first show was a blast. The place was full of happy dancing people. The Clash were more than your average, good-time band: you not only had a good time but you also thought about issues that bothered people. Things were serious and there was a lot to be angry about, but there was also a lot to have fun about.

It was a little difficult for me because I didn't understand the words at first, and I knew the words were very important and powerful. And there were certain points where the audiences in England would be powerfully singing along with a couple of lines, but I had no idea what they were singing.

The force of the music made it sound like a battlefield, a Clash: the lights were always flashing, like explosions.

**The Sunday flea market in Sausalito, northern California.**

**Paul:** I found loads of bits and pieces there. Being a habitual Portobello marketer, Sausalito was quite novel, because the array of things on display was quite different. That jacket I'm wearing I'd got in America, for example.

**Bob:** My favourite time on that tour was when it was just me and the band in my little car, after we'd been to the Sausalito flea market. We drove to Mount Tamapais, in Mill Valley. It's a kind of disorienting place. You park your car and walk out into a field, and without you noticing the field starts to slant and turn sideways. And you're no longer in a field: you're on a path cut into the edge of a very steep hill. And on the left-hand side is a 500-foot drop. It's really this series of huge, very rounded, very steep hills. And you can just sit up there and see for miles and miles and miles, over the ocean or back inland.

**Caroline:** I was very happy for Bob to take them off whilst I was organising the press and getting ready for the gig. When you're working so hard you get a lot of reward just from the fact that it seems to all be succeeding.

They got to the gigs, the gigs were fantastic - once you could get the various people out of their rooms and onto the coach.

**Mick with Mikey Dread.**

**Paul:** Mikey got a shock when he first saw the snow. Because we first met him in Scotland - he came straight up there when his plane arrived from Jamaica. He came over to be on our tour, because we'd loved his records so much. He lives in Bristol now, where he has a radio show.

**Caroline:** Everybody was so thin because it was so difficult to get food. You'd finish the gig, and because of the intensity of their performance, when they got offstage they could hardly breathe for half an hour, lying flat out, getting their breath back. And despite the fact that there would be food backstage, it was at that point quite difficult to eat. So you'd get back in the coach, and you'd be driving all night. You might be able to snatch something at one of these supermarkets, but by the time you got to the hotel, where there was good food, everyone was too exhausted to eat it. Everybody got very, very thin.

**Paul:** I remember Joe and I were staying in this hotel, and absolutely starving. So we ordered two pizzas, but we didn't realise how enormous they were going to be - we thought we were going to get two little English pizzas. Anyway, they lasted a couple of days.

**Bob:** They'd been on tours in England where you just have a mini-bus. But they'd never been on a tour bus where you have your own bunk. And that was kind of a luxury and I think they liked it. The bus would have a good sound system, and you had somewhere to lie down when you had a five or eight-hour ride. But it's not like having a hotel bed - you don't really sleep much - but you can pass out for a while. If you're on it for a few weeks, you just go and lie down, and you're in these little coffin-sized compartments, trying to

figure out if it's better for your feet or your head to be forward. And then it's just this constant diesel sound. But it's like travelling in your bedroom, like being in the house with people with the same sense of humour and the same sensibility.

Because I knew the scene I was probably useful to have around. They'd constantly ask me about local customs: 'Do we leave a tip for these people?' 'Yes.' 'Is it okay to buy that kind of garbage food in a place like this?' 'No, don't!' Or: 'How come this beer doesn't get you high?' 'Because there is not much alcohol in it.' Little American questions like that.

**David Johansen:** We went on the road at the same time around America. We would talk on the CB on our buses. And I remember sometime we were in the middle of nowhere, and we each had reviews of the others' shows, and we would get on the CB and read denigrating reviews of each other's shows to each other. Mainly that was me and Joe: we had similar reactions to things.

**Annie Liebowitz takes pictures of the band backstage at Santa Monica Civic Centre.**

**Caroline:** No doubt they are giving her a hard time because she is press.

Mick: Fantastic, that night, wasn't it? That was the first time we played in LA, at the Santa Monica Civic.

**Joe:** Rodney Bingenheimer! You've got to have him in there... he's an important cultural figure! He supported a lot of new bands.

Paul talks to Stiv Bators

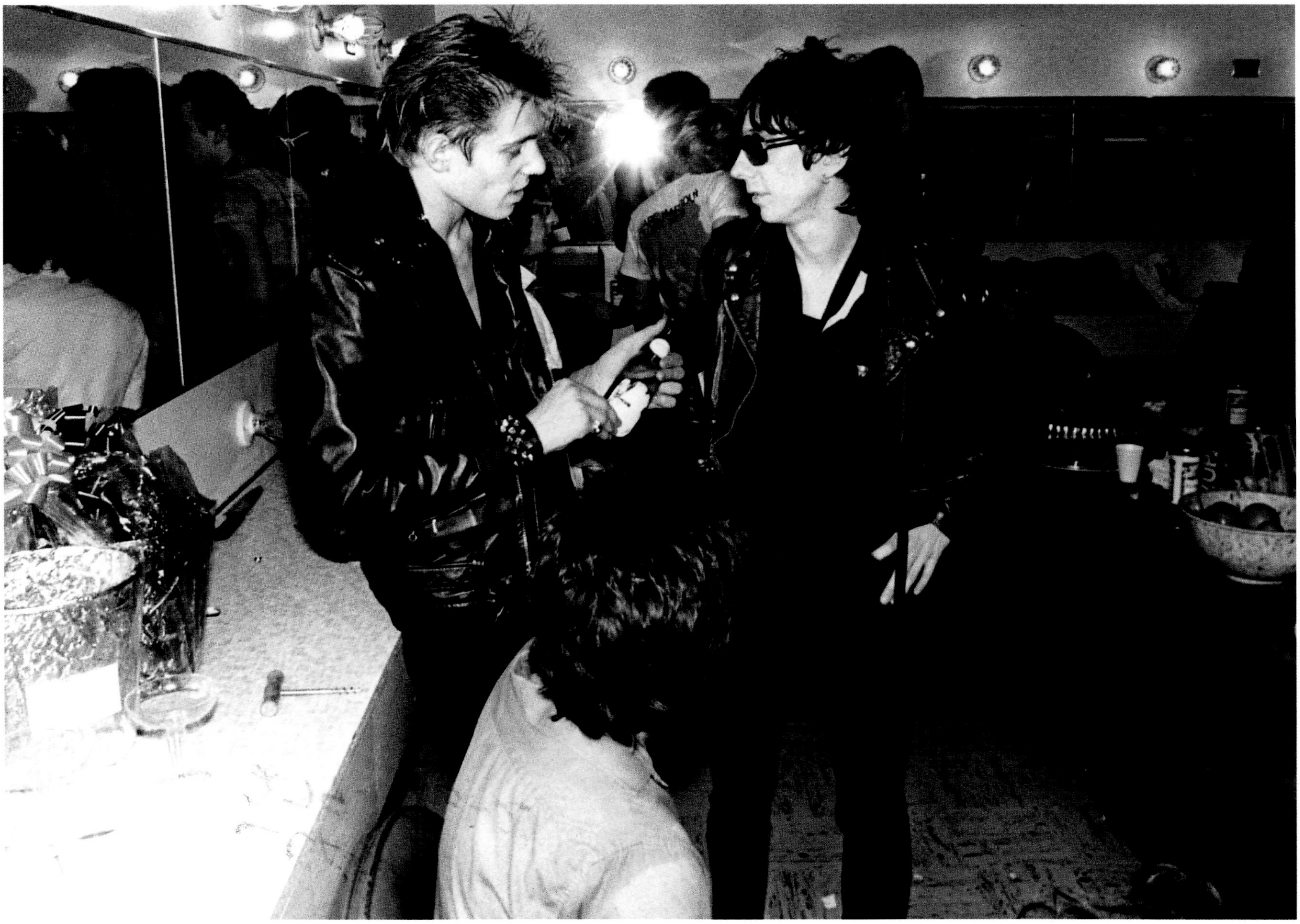

**Joe:** Not lost in the supermarket.

**Paul:** Caroline has made the wise move of choosing the centre checkout counter (bottom right), knowing the hold-up that's going to happen with us lot. We're hoping that all the stuff stored under our jackets doesn't get noticed.

**Mick:** Cherry aid. Root beer. And milk and a cake. That's what I've got: that's about right. Really foul.

**Paul:** That looks a bit frightening (top right). I'd be worried if I were that cashier. It looks as though Topper is about to hit her on the head, just as she's opening the cash-till.

**Caroline:** It's the biggest truck stop in the world, somewhere outside of Amarillo, Texas: thousands of these big rigs, and a one-street town with a wooden boardwalk, and houses with wooden facades and double-swing doors. Everybody by this time was wearing cowboy boots and spurs, so when they are walking down the boardwalk, the spurs are literally clinking as though it's a western movie, and everybody is completely into this. So they swing open the doors of this place. It's a massive great barn of a place with wooden tables, and a piano in a corner, and a long bar where the dudes are all lined up drinking their cold beer. And as they walk in, a hush falls, as this gang of English rock'n'rollers walks in. And the first thing they see is a stuffed Red Indian, and there are scalps hanging from the walls and a great bison's head. It immediately feels like a little bit of a dangerous situation. Luckily we have the drivers with us. So we sit down at these trestle tables, and on the menu is rattlesnake, which we all had. But we didn't hang about.

**Paul:** God, that was horrendous. I couldn't believe that place. This was somewhere like Oklahoma. We drove from LA to St Louis, and it's somewhere along there. It was real redneck country. Note the whip on the table.

**Mick:** You always get cowboy hats when you go over there if you're English. I went to the Grand Ole Opry once. I went to the original place in Nashville, but they'd moved the Grand Ole Opry out of town and you go on a bus. Everyone is in polyester, looking at you in your cowboy hat, obviously being an English person.

**Paul:** Caroline said, 'Who do you want to come on tour with you in America?' And, as a joke really, because we thought it would be impossible, we said, 'Oh, Bo Diddley!' And she tracked him down in Australia, where he was playing, and came back to us and said, 'Bo Diddley's on the tour.' We couldn't believe it: suddenly he was on the bus with us.

I remember when I was staying at Joe's squat: he used to have all these album covers with no records in them. There was a lot of Ronnie Hawkins and Bo Diddley, and I was familiar with the Bo Diddley stuff. And you'd go enthusiastically to hear this record, except it wasn't there in the sleeve. So you'd sit and stare at the album cover.

**Caroline:** I went to the American record company and said that we needed money for Bo Diddley to come on tour with us. They said, 'Bo Diddley? You can't tour with Bo Diddley. He'll be canned off the stage: you're touring through the southern States, and he'll be canned offstage.' I said, 'In that case we will definitely want Bo Diddley on tour with us.' I explained what the record company had said to the band, and so to make sure Bo Diddley wasn't dissed at any of the shows, Joe went out before Bo Diddley's set and introduced him.

However, Bo Diddley would not go onstage unless he had his money in his pocket. So before every performance I had to go to Wells Fargo Bank and pick up $10,000 in cash and give it to

him. And every night Bo Diddley played with The Clash he had a $10,000 wad of cash in his back pocket.

He did most of the tour. It cost so much money that that was why The Clash didn't make any profit: the support act was getting three times as much as The Clash were getting at each gig.

By the third gig we realised he had not played any of his old classic tunes. He was playing new stuff. And so Joe asked me to go and ask him if he would play some of his old classic hits - which was very funny, because at that point The Clash were refusing to play White Riot, and all the fans were coming to me and saying, 'Could you please ask Joe to play White Riot?' And

Strummer was saying, 'Nah. I'm never going to play that song again!'

So I did go to Bo Diddley and said that we really admired some of his early songs: would he mind playing them? And he said, 'I'm not going to play any of my early songs. I don't own the copyright to those early songs. I was ripped off with them all. So I'm only going to play what I own.' But I think The Clash eventually played White Riot.

**Mick:** Look at Bo Diddley's case for his square guitar - it's custom-built, no doubt.

**Paul:** Bo introduced us to this amazing drink he'd have before he went onstage - rock and rye, which contained fruit inside the bottle. He used to drink it for his throat - or so he said. I'm surprised there's not a bottle lurking somewhere - I don't see one...

Caroline: Bo is telling us stories, and one of these concerns how he is so sure there is going to be nuclear Armageddon that he has built a shelter, absolutely stocked to the hilt with canned food.

**Barry (Scratchy) Myers, The Clash's favourite DJ from London, accompanied them on the road:**
I was resident DJ at Dingwalls in London. The Clash played four nights at the Music Machine in Camden, and I was the DJ on two of them. One of those nights, Johnny Green came up to me and said that Joe really liked what I was playing, and added, 'And I do too.'

I was asked to do an entire UK tour with them, in late 1978. I was playing punk rock from The Ramones to the Pistols, Iggy and the Dolls and the MC5, reggae and ska, r'n'b and rockabilly, and Sixties soul. It was attitude music.

Then I did the first US tour. They were blowing audiences away on that. They'd never seen anything like it. The Clash playing these large venues was very much setting their own standards - groups like The Ramones and Patti Smith meant much more in England than in America. Everywhere they went, the response was incredible. We went over there with very much a cocky English attitude. I think they broke the mould by taking over their entire crew. CBS couldn't believe it: it was that whole sense of The Last Gang in Town.

**Paul:** We always used to start up the show with the same kind of music we played at home. I loved that spaghetti western music that we'd often start a show with.

**Caroline:** These are Simonon's fantastic tapes, which were later stolen.

**Paul:** I used to make a lot of tapes. But I got a CD burner recently, which is brilliant. It's like having a shop.

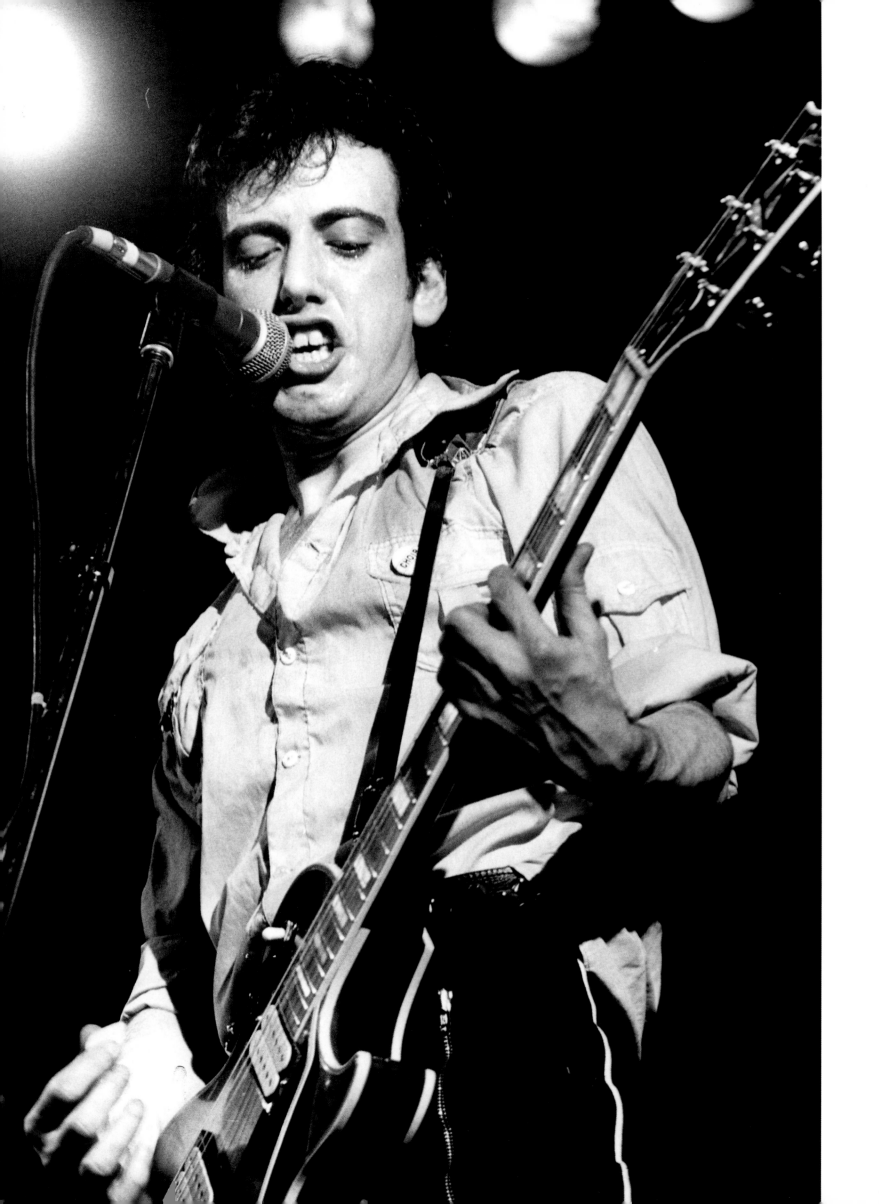

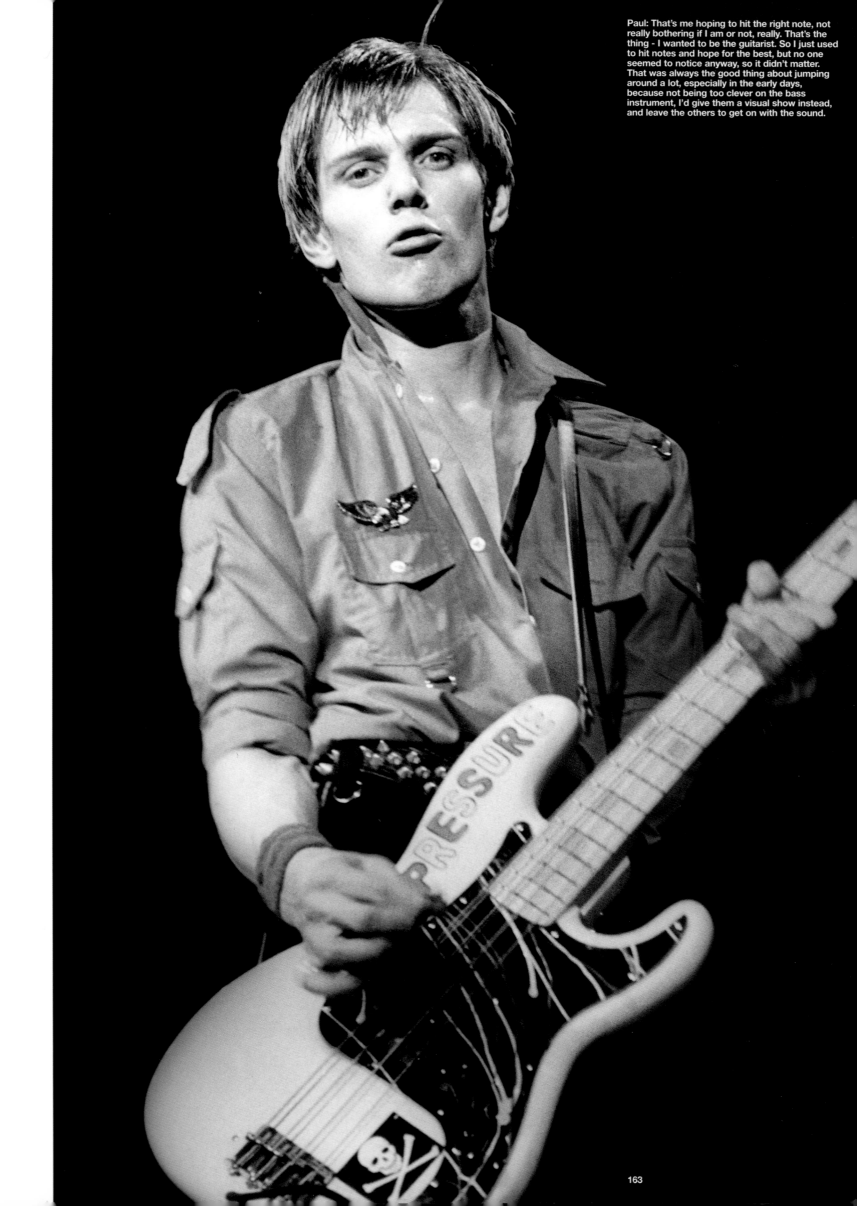

Paul: That's me hoping to hit the right note, not really bothering if I am or not, really. That's the thing – I wanted to be the guitarist. So I just used to hit notes and hope for the best, but no one seemed to notice anyway, so it didn't matter. That was always the good thing about jumping around a lot, especially in the early days, because not being too clever on the bass instrument, I'd give them a visual show instead, and leave the others to get on with the sound.

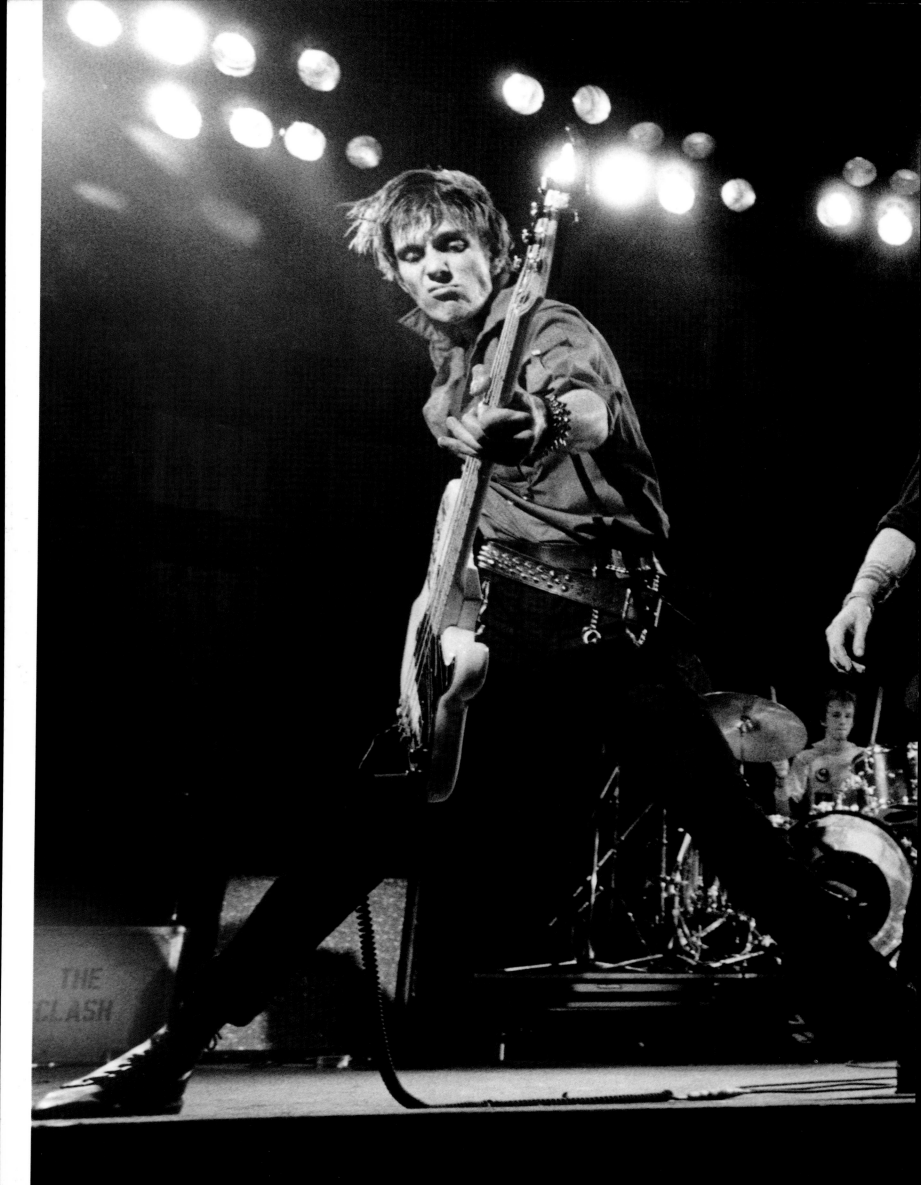

David Johansen, Debbie Harry and piano player Al Fields in the group's dressing room after their show at the Palladium in New York, 1979.

David Johansen: I thought The Clash were a good band. They were good guys. They weren't full of shit: they didn't take it too seriously. I knew Joe especially. I could always sit and talk with Joe.

Assorted celebrities with The Clash after the
Palladium show: the ubiquitous Andy Warhol,
Susan Blond (Epic Records publicity vice-
president), guitarist Lenny Kaye and John Cale.

**Pati Giordano took this picture of Bob working the dressing room.**

**Susan Blond:** Bob is the only photographer to get The Clash to stay still for him for a second. And the photographs are evidence why: he managed to capture their attitude, their brilliance and their gorgeous faces, as no one else could.

Joe talks to Nico.

Mick: My mum, 'cos she lived in the States, used to send me Creem magazine and Rock Scene magazine. Rock Scene magazine was how I got into a lot of things.

Bob: I took pictures for Rock Scene; it was the first American magazine to show British punk.

**Bob:** In December 1979 I took off to London because I had a place to stay at photographer Sheila Rock's house. Blondie and Richard Hell were touring and I knew The Clash were there. Christmas I spent with The Clash at Acklam Hall. Mick was saying that nobody had anything to do on Christmas Day in England. So The Clash said, 'Come out and have some fun with us for a couple of hours.' And it was just amazing that they went to a little local neighbourhood place. They were playing pretty big halls by that time, and that week they were on a major bill at Hammersmith Odeon, a big, ornate old theatre.

The Clash seemed to enjoy it even more at Acklam Hall. It was much more the band's style. They liked to keep it real like that.

I saw the bugle at Paul's house before the show at Acklam Hall. I went to Paul's place to go to the show and there was a bugle sitting on the table. I picked it up and started to play it, and Paul came running in: 'Oh, you know how to play? We were trying to get Baker to do it but he couldn't manage.'

Bob Gruen opens the show playing a bugle at Notting Hill's Acklam Hall on Christmas Day, 1979.

**Mick:** That was a tradition started by the Sex Pistols when they went to play in Huddersfield. Christmas Day is a really good day to do things. We played Christmas Day and Boxing Day. Christmas wasn't as packed, but by Boxing Day you couldn't move. And I'd seen the 101ers with Joe at the Acklam Hall.

**Kosmo Vinyl:** The Westway to The Clash is what Trenchtown was to The Wailers - a physical and spiritual place. The idea to play at Acklam Hall on Christmas and Boxing Day was to do something for the community from which they came. It was home. Mick, Joe and Paul walked not very far to the gig, which was held at the old socialist community centre.

It was 50p to get in, the same as it cost to get into the youth club. It wasn't leaked. The posters didn't go up until the pubs had shut on Christmas Eve. It was just an idea to give a Christmas present in the form of music for the extended family in the neighbourhood: for the hood, for the yard, for the manor. There was a poster and you got a ticket and a badge. Mind you, the roadies never forgave me for making them work on Chrismas Day.

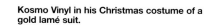
Kosmo Vinyl in his Christmas costume of a gold lamé suit.

**Bob:** There was a two-day benefit concert for Cambodia at the Hammersmith Odeon. I remember The Who and Wings were the headliners. The Pretenders played, and Ian Dury among others, and The Clash played the same day as The Who.

I'm glad Kate Simon took a shot of me opening The Clash set. After the show there was a big, very private party for the musicians. As I walked in with Mick Jones, the publicist said I was 'press' and couldn't come in - but Mick said I played in the band and insisted I be allowed in with him.

**Paul:** The great thing about Pete Townshend was that from early on he came to our concerts, and one time he even played onstage with us - I think Steve Jones also played at the same time with him, in Brighton.

**Steve Jones also played onstage with you at Manchester Free Trade Hall: there were rumours he was going to replace Mick...**

**Paul:** There was lots of weird stuff going around at that time. There had been talk about me meeting Malcolm McLaren, as a replacement for Sid. So I was supposed to meet Malcolm with Bernie - but I didn't turn up. I didn't really take it seriously, to be honest.

**Mick backstage with Chrissie Hynde at the Hammersmith Odeon Cambodia concert.**

Musician Patti Paladin adjusts Joe's look as photographer Kate Simon looks on.

**Mick:** That's really lovely: Guy Stevens. He started Mott the Hoople, and I followed them around the country when I was younger - I used to go anywhere to see them. So because of that we got on fantastically - I trusted him. Pretty soon after this picture was taken he died. Kosmo looks fantastic too.

**Paul:** It's good you can tell Guy obviously has been sitting in beer.

Joe with Ian Dury, who played the same night as The Clash and The Who.

Paul: Ian was a funny character. I remember going to his house a couple of times, and each time the music for entertainment was a live broadcast of the Horseguards Parade, which happens on the Queen's birthday. You'd be having a conversation with the sound of brass bands and soldiers marching in the background.

The Clash
LONDON CALLING
Two For A Fiver! On Album Or Cassette
BUY YOUR COPY HERE
The Clash
LONDON CALLING
The Clash
records
and tapes
discount

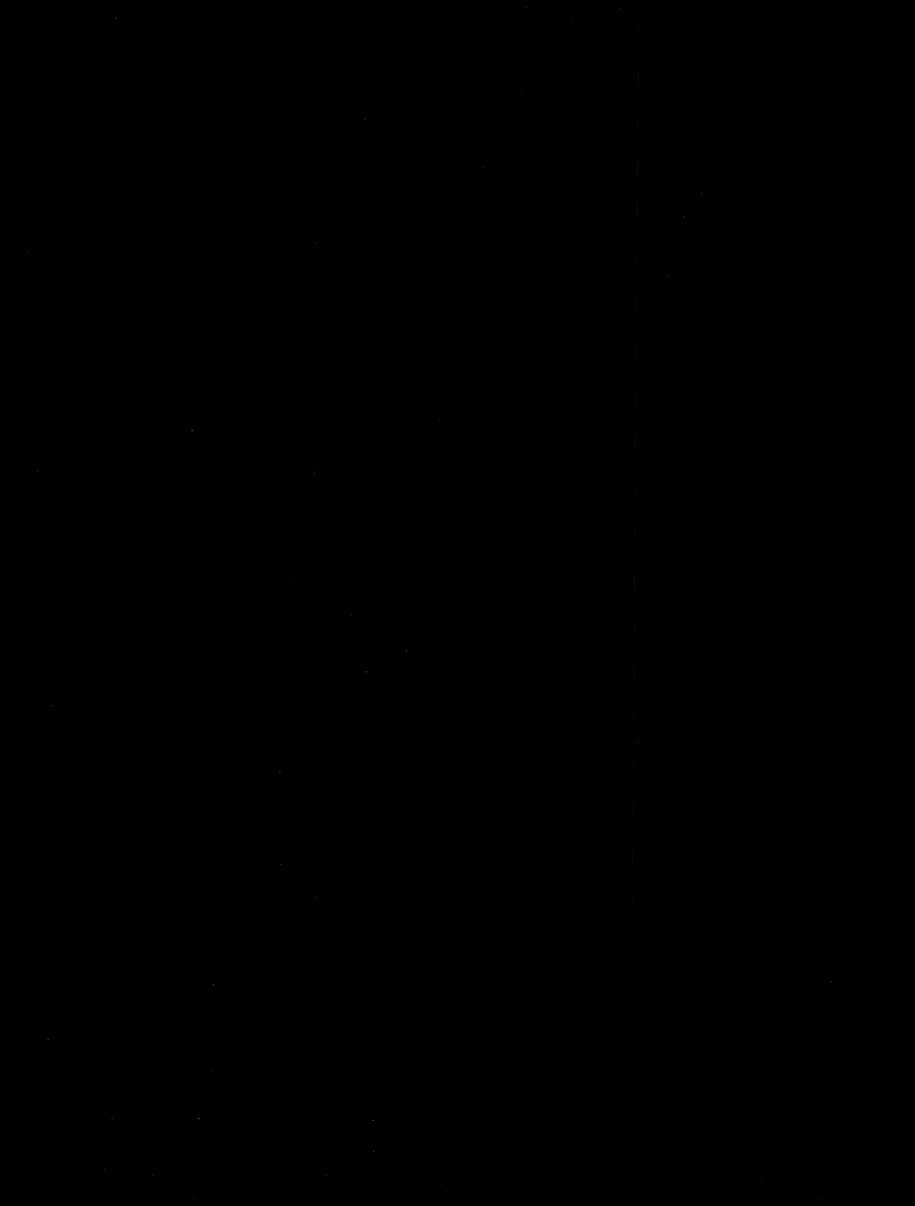

In March 1980 The Clash came back to
the USA with Mikey Dread and the great
New Orleans legend Lee Dorsey.

EGYPTIAN

APOCALYPSE NOW

Mick: I remember when Apocalypse Now opened, I went to see it on the first day in LA, at that big Cinerama cinema on Sunset in Hollywood.

As well as performing his own set, Mikey Dread would join The Clash during Bankrobber and Armageddon Time.

**The pool of the Sunset Marquis in West Hollywood.**

**Bob:** I remember when Mick arrived there, he walked into the lobby, dropped his bags and called out, 'Honey, I'm home.'

**Mick:** Everybody hangs out by the pool - it's so great. I've been ot the Lido a few times in London, and you go into shock just getting in the water, it's so cold. But this was so warm.

Famed New Orleans producer and performer
Lee Dorsey traveled with The Clash and was
their opening act.

**Paul:** Lee Dorsey was really entertaining, a no-nonsense character. Someone had once given him a hard time in a bar, so he'd taken his revolver and shot him in the foot.

Tour bus as Club House.

**Paul:** I don't like the look of Mick's bedroom.

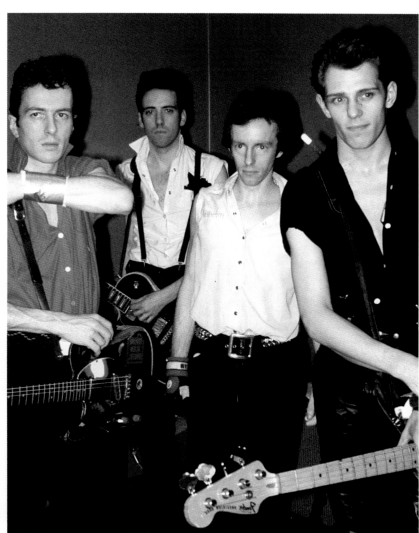

Top right: For the London Calling tour, Mickey
Gallagher, keyboards player with Ian Dury and
the Blockheads, played with The Clash onstage.

**Joe:** Hats can really keep you together on the road. In the background you can see Jonesy, I think perhaps feeling airsick. As travellers in America, we hunted down bowling jackets with a passion, since they were considered very exotic. I still feel the same way about them.

Mick didn't always travel well.

Reading the reviews from the night before, at the airport.

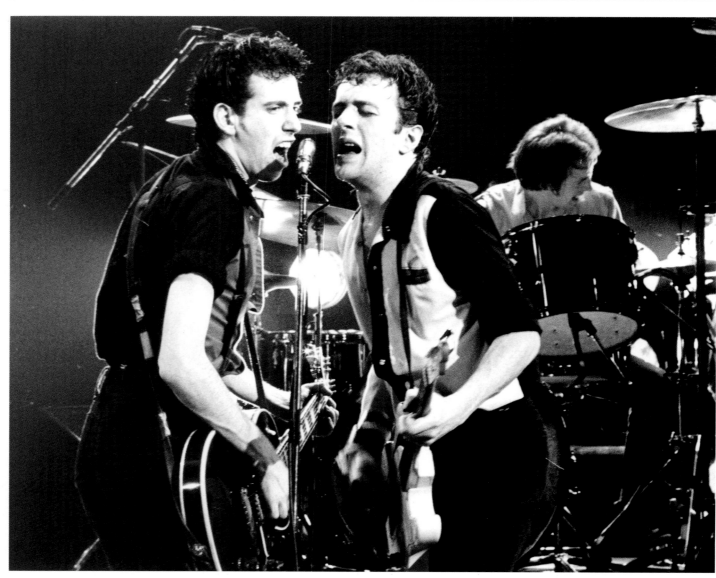

**Mick with Lisa Robinson; Joe with Johnny Thunders; Debbie Harry and Chris Stein.**

**Paul:** The first time we met Johnny Thunders in New York, he had those motorcycle boots. And Bob took us to the shop where they sold them, an army surplus store. Then we used to wear them all the time, to the point where in England people used to refer to them as Clash boots. But what's really strange about those boots is the way that the hair on your legs gets worn away by them.

**Bob was always ready to race off to get another roll of film developed...**

**Joe:** You've got to have that in. As punters we want to know what's going on and who's behind the camera.

This was the overnight queue for tickets when The Clash announced they were to play six dates at Bonds nightclub in Times Square, Manhattan.

Don Letts: In the late 70s the two sevens clashed; in the early 80s two cities clashed - London and New York. We'd just come out of the Punk Rock thing, a time in which we believed that if you didn't stand for something, you'd fall for anything. It was with this same ethos that The Clash took New York in 1981 playing at Bonds in Times Square, and I was there to capture it all on celluloid. Joe, Paul, Mick and Topper came, saw, conquered and embraced the city with an epic sixteen-show back-to-back stint that was to see the punk ethic live, loud and direct. The crowd came to see a rock show; what they got was a sonic culture clash that would pre-empt many of the most interesting musical moves today. Interspersed with The Clash, who drew fast and shot straight, were acts like Grandmaster Flash and Lee Perry, both culturally miles away from the American rock massive. It can't be denied that these musically challenging shows got mixed reviews. There were riots in the streets, club wars, and news flashes on the TV and for a moment it seemed like the city was brought to its knees.

You could love or hate The Clash but they could not be ignored.

What left a lasting impression on me was the way NYC adopted The Clash as the city's soundtrack that summer. Black American boom boxes, Hispanic low-riders, WBLS radio, the emerging graffiti crews and B-boys were all grooving to The Clash. The Magnificent Seven rocked the block.

**Bugle-blowing from Bob began each encore at Bonds.**

**Paul:** Bonds was really exhausting, because of the situation with the fire department. All the shows just merged into one: it was definitely exhausting. For Joe it was really difficult having to sing practically every night. It was sixteen gigs. It was a difficult period for us, because the record company weren't behind the album, Sandinista.

**How had they evolved by the time they were playing Bonds?**

**Bob:** Bonds was a big thing because it seems that the bigger a group gets the more distant they get from their audience. But the bigger The Clash got the more they wanted to do for their audience and give back. The Clash don't walk by people on the streets or ignore them: if somebody says hello to them, they'll say hello back, and ask them what they are thinking and what is going on. And they'd genuinely want to know and be in touch with people. At Bonds when it really got out of hand and the promoter had oversold the shows, instead of refunding half the money they said, 'Well, if we sold twice the number of tickets, we'll just play twice the number of shows.' What band does that for the same money? Plus throw in a couple of matinees for the kids, where they had the Brattles, a band of 8-year-old kids, opening for them.

**The Bonds dates seemed to cement their status in the USA...**

**Bob:** It was a funky place. It wasn't a theatre; it was outside the usual theatre sort of shows. A former men's department store, with a linoleum floor and beams and a makeshift stage.

One thing that was fascinating was the way they intertwined the culture of hiphop, breakdancing and graffiti - which was going on live in Times Square outside Bonds - into the group.

They'd met Fab Five Freddie and Futura 2000 and a few of the other graffiti artists and they were really interested in that aspect of things: the people who were involved in the underground and other art forms. The group all had an art background. They all had input into things like that, and they were all more comfortable downtown than going to fancy restaurants uptown.

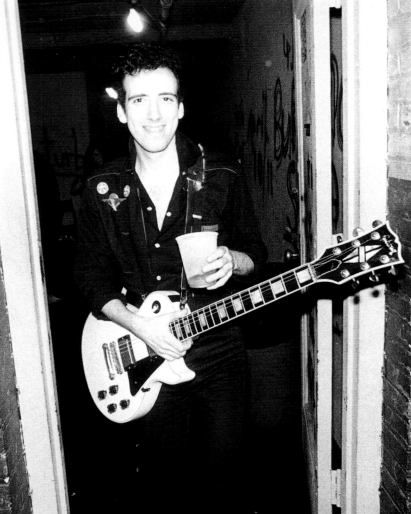

**David Johansen:** I went to Bonds, because of this band on called The Brattles - a lot of my girlfriends' kids were in it. Bonds was a good scene: they did daytime shows for the kids, which was the one I went to.

**Bernard:** Because of Bonds the public became interested in hip-hop. I endeavoured to get those groups on like Grandmaster Flash; not that most of the audience liked them. But that led to a helluvalot.

**The Bonds shows were to promote the three-record album Sandinista.**

**Joe:** We'd probably gone in about 36 different directions on Sandinista. We'd tried things we weren't sure we could do... after a while it became apparent that we were beginning to sit on a pile of tracks. So we thought, let's see how far we can push 'em - CBS, that is - as far as price goes. Originally we were intending just to make the usual double, and we weren't bothered about counting the tracks. And then we found it was gonna be a jam fitting it all on a treble, a tight fit.

**At Bonds the dressing-room was littered with pink bags from Trash and Vaudeville, the retro clothing store on St Mark's Place.**

**Paul:** It was so cheap and the stuff you could buy was so different from what you'd get in London: it was a real good find for us.

**Kosmo Vinyl:** What happened to The Clash at Bonds was that they got phenomenal media coverage. Bill Graham called me at the Gramercy Park and said, 'You're on every channel: you've got more coverage than Woodstock got!' Up to this time the coverage of punk was safety pins and Sid and Nancy. So this was a very positive thing. I think the riot in Times Square did it.

Ultimately, Bernie and I didn't realise the consequences of setting up a new venue in New York and how many people's noses were going to be put out of joint. We were just thinking of The Clash and their audience. But there were millions of dollars involved for these other venues, so they weren't going to let us go quietly about our business.

The thing is that the coverage was mind-bogglingly huge. After Bonds The Clash went from being a force to be reckoned with in our own eyes, to one that everyone recognised.

The record company were banned from the gig, because they'd done nothing to support Sandinista. So you've got the biggest media event going and CBS have to say, 'We can't help you: contact Kosmo at the Gramercy.' They learned a lesson there. It put The Clash on the map for real, big-time brand recognition. We clawed our way into the Premier Division with that one. It would have been a landmark event if we'd just played the original seven days.

The audience reaction to rap on the first night was of major importance, presenting rap music to a white audience. And - horribly - the response was awful. I had to go to Grandmaster Flash and apologise. We didn't realise that these white audiences would hate these acts, and boo them and throw things. And after Grandmaster Flash had had that reaction, I knew the Treacherous 3 and the Funky Four would get the same response. Even The Fall played at Bonds. What an event!

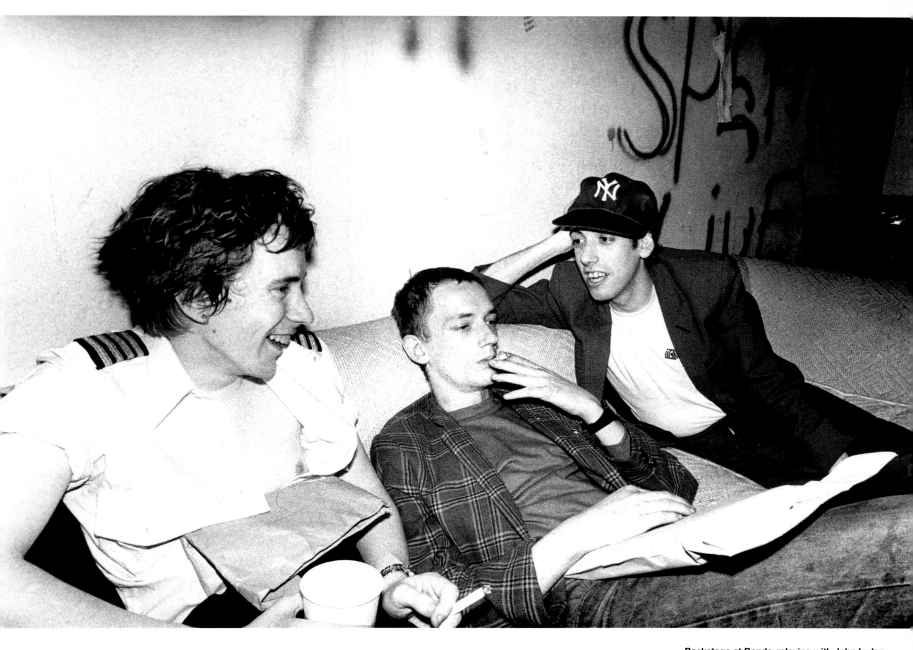

Backstage at Bonds, relaxing with John Lydon and Keith Levene of Public Image Ltd: Lydon had just moved his life to New York.

Battery Park on Manhattan. Don Letts, who as a DJ had introduced punks at London's Roxy club to reggae, directs his cameraman in the filming of 'Clash on Broadway', a documentary that eventually went missing.

**Don Letts:** During this period I also directed the 'Rock the Casbah', 'Radio Clash' and 'Should I Stay Or Should I Go' videos which I rate amongst my finest work, and it is with an immense sense of pride that I can say I worked with The Clash. They say memories were meant to fade, that they were designed that way; well, thank God for Bob Gruen.

**Bob:** The RCA building is my favourite place to go to take pictures in New York, because you get the Empire State Building and the World Trade Center in the picture. They were in the building for a TV show and I took them upstairs to see the view.

**Mick:** We played the Tom Snyder Show with Futura 2000 doing graffiti behind us. I think it was quite good; Joe said some things about squatting - they didn't know what squatting was. Joe roughed up Tom Snyder's teddy-bear - which was a mascot for the programme - by sticking Clash stickers all over it.

**Mick:** Really on top of the world.

The great Beat poet Allen Ginsberg with the great punk group The Clash at Electric Ladyland Studio in New York, recording Combat Rock in December 1981.

Asbury Park, New Jersey, June 1982.

**Paul:** It was quite funny, that period, because fans would come backstage and sit around and suddenly have their hair cut: they'd have drinks, talk to the band, then get a haircut.

Busloads of media were brought down from
nearby Manhattan for a press conference with
The Clash when they played at Asbury Park;
afterwards this was followed by a lavish
press party in the amusement park there.

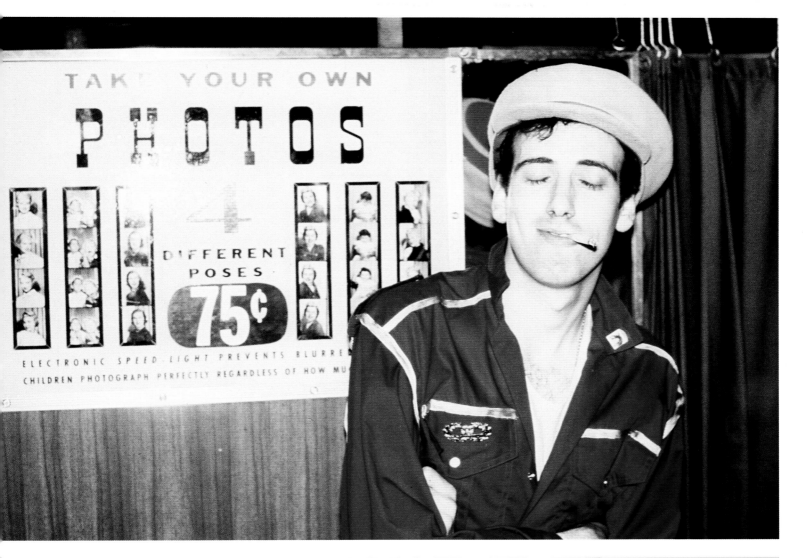

The Clash in the mirror maze after the show at Asbury Park, New Jersey.

Futura, Bob and Fab Five Freddy.

The Combat Rock tour marked The Clash's
sleeveless shirts period. They played Manhattan's
Pier in pouring summer rain. Jamaican reggae
superstar Gregory Isaacs played the first of the
two nights, but didn't turn up for the second
show. Allen Ginsberg was there at both shows to
recite his poetry.

Mick Jones with the former singer from
Generation X, about to reinvent himself as
Billy Idol, punk superstar.

Kosmo Vinyl in archetypal moody pose.

Mick with Lisa Robinson and promoter
Ron Delsener.

**Bernard Rhodes:** I had an idea and it ended up as punk. It was something I put together. It was my idea. I make a point of being where the action is. I am one of the most creative people in the world. I'm embarrassed a lot by what's taking place. I cut the ice. Did the pathway. The Clash let themselves down. The idea was to have punk so horrible and bad that the record companies couldn't rip it off. The kids didn't understand the very creative artistic statement that was being made. I want to be the mystery man, not the bogey man - I want to be Roy Orbison, not Gary Glitter.

**Joe:** Bernie lost control of us. His scene was not to give us any money in case it ruined us, which is the way you deal with kids - which he thought we were. But he underestimated us. Like people say; Bernie wrote our songs, but that's not true at all. All he said was, 'Don't write love songs, write something that you care about, that's real.' And it's a pity we fell out with him cos we made a good team.

But he got really funny when The Clash all started to happen. We wouldn't see him from week to week. If he wanted to communicate he'd just send a minion - inferring he was too busy elsewhere to deal with us.

You know Complete Control, which Mick wrote about the record company. In fact we got the phrase off Bernie one night in that pub in Wardour Street, The Ship. I remember him going - he'd obviously been talking to Malcolm and was trying to be the master puppeteer - going, 'Look, I want complete control, I want complete control'. And we were just laughing at him.

**Bernard:** The thing about Bob is that he's a fan. But I'm not a fan: I'm just someone who's very disappointed.

Band manager Bernard Rhodes, mouthpiece Kosmo Vinyl, Clash merchandise magnate Sean Carasov and administrative assistant Peta.

Paul: It felt a bit like miming, because there were so many people there. And the audience wasn't allowed to be very close, so you didn't really get the same reaction from them. It was fantastic, but everyone seemed a bit distanced from each other - in clubs the group and audience would feed off each other.

**A long way from Acklam Hall...**

**Did you get nervous at a vast show like that?**

**Paul:** Not really: you'd get more nervous in a small club, because the audience were just there in front of you. And at these stadium shows you knew exactly what you were supposed to be doing, so there was no need to get nervous. You would feel a slight jitter, but as soon as you started playing that went away. And also not having anything to eat helped as well. But then you'd come offstage and all the restaurants would be shut.

**Joe:** Terry Chimes (our original drummer) in action here at JFK Stadium. I'm sporting the trousers that started the camo craze. Kosmo's looking dapper and that's Lisa Robinson (NY writer, scene-maker) in the background.

**Joe:** Underneath the stands, waiting for the off signal. I can tell what I'm thinking - I'm thinking, 'Where's my hat now that I REALLY need it?' Or perhaps not - at this stage I was into Daniel Boone.

Pete Townshend, guitarist with the billtopping
Who, and Mick Jagger, whose daughter Jade
had nagged him to go to the show because she
was a Clash fan.

**Mick and Joe visit backstage with David Johansen.**

**David Johansen:** When I was a kid, I was a street kid, and I got that same vibe from Joe - we spoke the same language, a certain kind of innate intelligence about the beast, and feeding its face. All those fuckers want to make you a star, but you're nothing more than a racehorse to them. And Joe had an awareness about that corporate structure. And making music and not being co-opted by it is an art form in itself. And Joe had that art. The people who can walk that tightrope are the ones who're interesting. He did it well: there's probably only about twenty people who've ever done it well.

**Joe checks his gear.**

287

**Paul:** Because of the problem with the food situation on tour, me and Raymond (with Paul, bottom left) used to meet up in his hotel room and get some food cooking between us, which was how we survived. Once, when Peter Jenner was managing us, he came into our dressing-room in Scandinavia and gave everyone their wages, including me, proceeding around the room. When he'd finished I said, as a joke, 'Where's mine?' And Jenner said, 'Oh, sorry,' and immediately gave me another lot. Raymond clocked it, so we split the proceeds.

**Did it seem odd when Terry Chimes, the drummer from the first album, replaced Topper Headon for the Combat Rock tour?**

**Paul:** Yes. But he was a lot easier to deal with, because he wasn't 'ill', as they refer to Topper's drug problems. But the drumming wasn't as explosive: Terry is very matter-of-fact in his drumming.

**Was it traumatic when Topper left?**

**Paul:** Yeah. But suddenly you've got to go on tour and get on with it, really. If truth be known, it did start to drag us all down, Topper's drug thing.

**The Clash play Saturday Night Live.**

**Mick:** The spectacles were only clear glass.
Didn't affect my eyesight in any way.

**Joe:** Looks like it's a bad hat day on Fifth Avenue.

**Joe:** Waiting around at Saturday Night Live - somebody had the idea to stop in the midst of playing Should I Stay or Should I Go and hold a ghetto blaster up to the mike and play Rock The Casbah. Remember this is live TV; so the moment comes. I press the play button. Nothing comes out. I fling the blaster through the air - thank God Baker catches it before it brains a hapless audience member. We carry on. Reason for no sound from the blaster? That little piece of see-through leader tape at the front of every cassette reel.

**The Clash prepare for the Shea Stadium show.**

**Bob:** I was very excited that my three favourite bands of all time played Shea Stadium on the same bill.

SHOW RUNNING ORDER
DAVID JOHANSEN 7-7:30 PM
CLASH 8-8:50 PM
WHO 9:30-11:45 P

**Paul:** I never really had a proper talk with him. He never seemed like a very verbal person. He didn't seem altogether there, in some ways.

The Clash played on November 1982 at the Bob Marley Festival in Montego Bay, Jamaica.

Paul: It wasn't just rock acts, it was reggae too. We had Peter Tosh before us, and before him was Black Uhuru. Didn't it rain? We ended up going on at four in the morning. I remember Peter Tosh complaining that it hadn't rained for that heathen group. The audience was a combination of Jamaicans and people who had come over from America. The Grateful Dead played. It was called the Bob Marley Festival and was the opening of a venue named after him in Montego Bay.

**Mick:** We went out into the festival and bought mushroom tea and were all tripping out.

**Bob:** Joe came back really happy because he'd traded a watch for a bag of pot worth about $5. I was supposed to be in Europe with Yoko Ono, but that got cancelled, and I came back to New York and immediately tried to go down to Jamaica. I travelled via Miami and ran into The Clash at the airport there.

Across the street from the gig there was this huge hotel and I went over and demanded a room. All I could get was a room that had been flooded with literally two inches of water on the floor. But the bed was above the water. They wouldn't let me sleep there the next night, so I ended up going down to the beach at five in the morning after the show ended and fell asleep on a deckchair. I woke up surrounded by kids and families. That show was the last time I saw The Clash play.

**Paul:** Most of our set was our reggae numbers. It was played on Jamaican radio, and they said the bass-player was really good, but the rest of the group was useless: they obviously couldn't get to grips with Mick's rock angle.

**Was reggae hard to play at first?**

**Joe:** I'm just talking about rhythm guitar. We couldn't play like the guys in Jamaica. So it was one chip. So I'd get into the rock steady... But I think it took us years before we could jam down on Armageddeon Time. It was like... jazz. I had a few licks I'd go back to. There was no plan: a bit of singing. Jam. Lovely. That was when we were really playing.

**Joe:** Our ghetto blasters were so cool even they wore hats! In the left photo, Digby wearing a Union army cap, and in the right photo Manu with Mohawk, staunch members of our road crew - in Jamaica for the festival.

Joe: Ahh! It's a long time since men wore hats! At the bar we see Simmo & Kosmo modelling a great pair of Stetsons. The best way to get in a bar brawl in London is to wear a hat like that. Ranking Roger (seated) and ourselves are in JA to play the Bob Marley Festival.

**Many thanks:**

Chris Charlesworth and Susan Currie at
Omnibus Press; Paul at Form; Virginia Lohle
of Star File.

Photography: Bob Gruen.
Editor: Chris Salewicz.
Art Direction and book design: Form®.
Creative Director: Kirk Teasdale.
Printed in Singapore.

The Clash first published in Great Britain in 2001
by Vision On publishing.

All photography © Bob Gruen
Book design © Form®

This edition published 2004 under exclusive
licence by Omnibus Press
(A Division of Music Sales Limited).

ISBN 1 903399 34 3
Order No: VO10131

The Author hereby asserts his/her right to be
identified as the author of this work in
accordance with Sections 77 to 78 of the
Copyright, Designs and Patents Act 1988.

All rights reserved. No part of this book may be
reproduced in any form or by any electronic or
mechanical means, including information
storage or retrieval systems, without permission
in writing from the publisher, except by a
reviewer who may quote brief passages.

Exclusive Distributors

Music Sales Limited,
8/9 Frith Street,
London W1D 3JB, UK.

Music Sales Corporation,
257 Park Avenue South,
New York, NY 10010, USA.

Macmillan Distribution Services,
53 Park West Drive,
Derrimut, Vic 3030,
Australia.

To the Music Trade only:

Music Sales Limited,
8/9 Frith Street,
London W1D 3JB, UK.

A catalogue record for this book is available
from the British Library.

Visit Omnibus Press on the web at
www.omnibuspress.com

01/05 (53509)